HAUS CURIOSITIES

These Islands

About the Author

Ali M. Ansari is a Professor of Modern History with reference to Iran at St. Andrews University in Scotland, where he is also the founding director of the Institute of Iranian Studies. He is a Fellow of the Royal Society of Edinburgh and a Senior Associate Fellow at the Royal United Services Institute. Ansari is the author of *Iran: A Very Short Introduction* and *Iran, Islam and Democracy*.

Ali M. Ansari

THESE ISLANDS

A letter to 'Britain'

HAUS
CURIOSITIES

First published by Haus Publishing in 2018
4 Cinnamon Row
London SW11 3TW
www.hauspublishing.com

A CIP catalogue record for this book is
available from the British Library

Print ISBN: 978-1-910376-98-0
Ebook ISBN: 978-1-912208-14-2

Typeset in Garamond by MacGuru Ltd

Printed in Spain

'But in any calculation about it one has got to take into account its emotional unity, the tendency of nearly all the inhabitants to feel alike and act together in moments of supreme crisis.'

– George Orwell, 'The Lion and the Unicorn'[1]

Contents

Acknowledgements

This Haus Curiosity has been longer in gestation than I would care to admit, drawn as it has been from my research, teaching and personal experiences over the past decade. In line with the series it aims to provide a contribution to the wider debate, and I hope readers will read it in the spirit in which it is intended. I am especially grateful to the many and varied readers who have taken the time to read through the draft and thought processes as they took shape – most obviously Peter Hennessy for having invited me to contribute to his series in the first place and for his helpful comments on the draft. In addition, Kevin Hague, Sam Taylor, Tom Holland, James Holland, Melanie Gibson, David Morgan, Chandrika Kaul and Charles Tripp were all kind enough to offer suggestions, corrections and clarifications, which I have sought to incorporate. My publishers, Barbara Schwepcke and Harry Hall, have been a huge encouragement, and my editor, Jo Stimpson, has been truly virtuous in her patience. Last and by no means least, I am grateful to my wife Marjon, whose ingenuity in challenging every premise of the piece has encouraged me to think, rethink and think again.

This is an interpretive essay on narratives and historical writing and presentation in both the academic and popular senses. It starts with an outline of 'Whig' history – the thesis – before turning to its critics – antithesis – and concludes with an assessment – synthesis. This approach by necessity will involve a degree of overlap as ideas and narratives are revisited, and arguments made. I hope nonetheless that any repetition serves to strengthen the overall argument and has been successfully kept to a minimum. It goes without saying that any errors are mine and mine alone.

Introduction

Why me?

A native of Iran and an historian of that country, I settled in the United Kingdom at the age of ten, from which time I developed an acute, if personal, appreciation of Britain. Born in Rome, educated in London, living and working in the Kingdom of Fife, I have long been comfortable with a multi-layered identity that complements and informs. I self-identify as British-Iranian. This essay represents my first attempt to address the question(s) of the country of my adoption, and my view is of one who stands at the crossroads of cultures. I take encouragement, in this otherwise daunting task, from the fact that being on the 'borderlands' has not precluded others from presenting their assessments of their adopted countries,[2] nor indeed prevented many excellent histories of Iran from being written by Britons. To paraphrase Kipling, what should they know of Britain who only Britain know?

Why do I write?[3]

A few years back, in the run-up to the referendum on Scottish independence, I went to dinner at the house of some close friends. Inevitably the issue of the referendum was raised along with broader questions about the value or otherwise of the British state. All of us agreed that 'Britain' had problems, but I stressed that I still considered my greatest – most treasured – possession to be my British passport. It is still unclear to me who was more surprised: my colleagues, who reacted to my statement with a mixture of puzzlement and surprise, or myself, being nonplussed by my colleagues' reaction. I quickly explained that the passport signified <u>security</u> and <u>stability</u> – a <u>refuge</u>, if you will, from an otherwise turbulent world – and that this in itself was an invaluable asset.

There was a time when British 'exceptionalism' in this particular respect was widely acknowledged. Long before people got used to berating the British Empire, many applauded British stability, the ability of the people of these islands to <u>govern</u> and indeed regulate themselves with such skill and efficiency and the fact that they had established what appeared to be an <u>organic</u> political <u>harmony</u> that was the envy of their revolutionary neighbours. It may have been less interesting – even a tad boring – but who needed interesting when the consequences of revolution were so disruptive? So comfortable and confident had Britain become in its political skin that it in fact became a refuge for both those escaping persecution and turmoil and, with no hint of irony, to revolutionaries from other countries – the most famous perhaps being Karl Marx.

The truth is that Britain has long been a refuge, even a sanctuary, for those fleeing persecution. Immigrants, and political refugees in particular, have long been part of the fabric of the British state and, one might add, the British sense of itself as the quintessentially 'liberal' state, both in its political definition and in terms of generosity of spirit. George Orwell considered the civilisation that characterised these islands as 'gentle' – a term that is ambiguous enough to be open to interpretation but is as good as any to convey the <u>essence</u> of a Britain that was comfortable, if not necessarily confident, in itself.[4] It should come as no surprise that these immigrants have often had a more acute appreciation of that essence than those who are native born, for whom the contradictions are all too apparent and the failings all too real.[5] Indeed, it is a fact that those who seek to define a community often come from its margins. It is at the political borders, the wider hinterland – the point of highest tension, if you will – that clarity can most easily be achieved, and is most enthusiastically pursued.

What's in a name?

To any visitor to these islands, one of the curiosities that will soon become apparent is the great difficulty in finding a collective noun that satisfies everyone or indeed works as a suitable descriptor. Orwell noted that there were six terms that were used, often interchangeably: 'England', 'Britain', 'Great Britain', 'the British Isles', 'the United Kingdom' and 'in very exalted moments, Albion'.[6] The use of 'Britain' and 'Great Britain' as shorthand for the United Kingdom remains problematic for those in Ireland (who of course have their own problems with nomenclature),[7] and an attempt in the late 19th century to encourage the use of the awkward-sounding 'United Kingdomers' not surprisingly failed to gain traction.[8] At the same time, while the Welsh came to accept 'Britain' and the Scots positively endorsed it[9] – it was after all in many ways their idea as a political term – the English have paradoxically always been reluctant adopters, preferring to use 'England' and 'English'.[10] Orwell, after all, while recognising the incongruity of usage, employed 'England' and 'Britain' interchangeably, with a tendency towards the former as indicated in the subtitle to his book *The Lion and the Unicorn: Socialism and the English Genius*. This tendency of the English, along with a proclivity to mock and/or diminish the contribution of the 'periphery', is (as Orwell was only too acutely aware) unsurprisingly a cause of some irritation among the non-English communities.[11]

It should come as little surprise that those on the margins were enthusiastic about the adoption of a more inclusive term; as noted, it is at the margins that nationalism comes into focus.[12] Minority communities have traditionally driven such processes, a good example being the Protestant Irish communities, who have been at the forefront of both defining Irish nationalism (Charles Stewart Parnell comes to mind) and identifying themselves closely with Britishness.[13] Even accepting the invented nature of identities, and their political expression in 'nations', there is no doubting the difficulty in reconciling the various terms to the satisfaction of all. It reflects in many ways the multi-layered and organic construction of the modern state; the process is one of a series of compromises being harmonised with greater or lesser success over time. But this harmonisation has proved by no means perfect, and the continued difficulty and lack of rationality has led some to conclude that the entire edifice is illegitimate. Much depends, of course, on how we define our terms.

Rethinking Britain (and the 'English')
It was not always thus. The reconciling of such terms becomes a problem when we ascribe them, and the need for them as

descriptors, to ethnicities, by which I mean groups of people tied and defined by a belief in a common kinship – a notion elevated by nationalist writers in the 19th century and beyond to the far more problematic concept of race. But in its original sense, and when the British state and 'nation' was being forged, an 'ethnick' connection denoted not a biological distinction, but rather an ideological one.[14] It was at that time more a matter of heritage and manners than kinship, and Englishness, for example, was a matter of character and values that could be acquired. The Scots, who bound themselves to England and the English after the 1707 Act of Union, understood the situation in this manner.[15] Consequently, David Hume's decision a few decades later to write *The History of England* rather than a history of Britain was not so incongruous as it might seem to our contemporary eyes.[16] 'England' was an idea that encapsulated a set of values belonging to all who chose to invest in it, and it remained largely unproblematic as a synonym for the whole of these islands until the late 19th century.[17] For their part, the English were only too well aware that they were a 'mongrel people' that defied definition by ethnicity but instead could and should be understood through language, character and manners – or, in our modern reading of the term, values.[18]

Viewed from the perspective of being unified by ideas, reconciliation becomes less problematic, and the friction that is bound to exist becomes part of a process. If we accept identities as inventions of history, products of historical experience, culture and heritage, reinforced through time and no less 'real' for that, they remain fluid and malleable to renewal, reinvention and connections of various types. So, too, does the idea of Britain: a geographic description reimagined as a political idea that could surmount, cement and complement the various identities that had settled on these islands. British-ness can be understood less as a distinct 'ethnicity' and more as a set of values and attitudes, a civic culture into which all invest and from which all draw, a 'common-wealth' of ideas. Inclusive rather than exclusive, it represents a binding layer on the dynamic, complex and occasionally fractious identities of these islands, providing for a composite – even, one might argue, hyphenated – identity: a commonwealth of the mind.[19] Perhaps, at this moment of supreme identity crisis, it is time to rediscover the emotional unity that lies at the heart of the idea of Britain.

The perils of Whig history

Contrary to popular perception, Britain is as much admired as resented abroad, with many external observers harbouring both views in equal measure (they are in some ways two sides of the same coin). This reflects the fact that the exercise of British policy frequently falls short of British ideals, though that might be expected given that ideals are always aspirational. But the British tendency to excessive self-deprecation, and at times self-condemnation, should not disguise the reality that others view Britain as a reference point against which many things are measured. This esteem for Britain may be grudging, and it may be reluctant, but it exists. European allies are perplexed by Brexit not because it's typical but because it does not match their expectation of us to be rational, measured and level headed. The British are acting, if you will, out of character. But this character is as much part of the European imagination as it is a reflection of the reality on these islands.

For example, during a visit to Italy shortly before the Scottish referendum in 2014, I was struck by the fawning admiration of my Italian colleagues for the wondrous liberalism of the British state, that it would be open to a referendum on its own dissolution and that it approached this existential moment with an air of matter-of-fact coolness. The British state was a voluntary association; the constituent parts could

leave if they wanted to, through the exercise of their demo-
cratic rights at the ballot box. My colleagues were in awe. No
such possibility existed in Europe, where the nation-state,
forged largely on the French revolutionary model, brooked
no such dissent. In Europe, the dominant model was not
'from the many, one', it was simply 'the one'.[20] We can perhaps
appreciate the value of my Italian colleagues' commentary
in light of recent experiences in Spain, but at the time I was
not convinced, arguing that on the contrary the British state
was being dangerously complacent about its future, and
that, for my part, I felt the fact that foreign nationals (EU
residents) could vote in such a crucial referendum, whereas
Scots resident elsewhere in the United Kingdom could not,
had crossed the line from a 'cool' laissez-faire to decadence.[21]

But Britain's approach to the referendum and the impression it made in Italy in many ways summed up the mythology of the British state both from within and without: that
on some fundamental level the British understand politics
and manage their political life well; that they understand the
power of consensus over coercion; and that the regulation of
state and society by the rigorous application of the rule of law
produces good, fair and above all stable governance. There
are many critics of the British state, and indeed those that
have been at the decidedly rough end of its exercise of power
will readily balk at such a presentation. Like all mythologies (and their associated narratives) this is undoubtedly a
varnished view – but, like all durable political mythologies,
it contains sufficient truth to gain traction with the public.
It has of course been subject to systematic deconstruction
and criticism for at least a century (this itself is a reflection

of the intellectual vibrancy that exists in Britain), and there are many learned individuals (self-taught or otherwise) who reject it, almost as a matter of honour. But before we turn to the critique, we should first remind ourselves of the main themes and narratives of what we can term 'the Whig reading' of British history.

The standard bearer of 'Whig history' was Thomas (Lord) Macaulay, whose *The History of England from the Accession of James the Second*, published in five volumes between 1848 and 1861, established the narrative frame of reference for English and by extension – given the period under review – British history. The focus on the Glorious Revolution of 1688 and its immediate aftermath, including the Union of 1707, was intended to provide a historical pedigree and political justification for the Whig party, which had dominated party politics for much of the 18th century. The Whigs remained an ideological force to be reckoned with throughout the 19th century, even as the party became subsumed and absorbed within the new (Peelite) Conservative and Liberal Parties. Macaulay sought to narrate a dramatic history, and he was criticised for excessive literary licence in embellishing his narrative for popular consumption. More critically, he was taken to task for providing an overtly ideological reading of history, smoothing out the rough edges to present a history of exceptional and, one might add, inevitable progress.

For Macaulay, the critical period in English history was that of the overthrow of James II in 1688 and the joint accession of William III, of Orange, and his wife Mary II, the eldest daughter of James II, who were invited to rule as co-monarchs by Parliament in a decision that retained the pretence of hereditary succession. This was far more than the establishment of a Protestant succession over James II's Catholic pretensions; this was the triumph of Parliamentary sovereignty over the absolutism of James II. This 'Revolution' was 'Glorious' because it restored the natural political order (applying the contemporary meaning of the word 'revolution'), and because in comparative terms it was considered relatively bloodless, though this view tended to ignore developments in Ireland and, perhaps more crucially, the bloody turmoil of the previous half century.

By way of compensation, perhaps, this period did oversee the definitive union of the Kingdoms of Scotland and England into a single Kingdom of Great Britain through a process of consensus rather than coercion, turning a dynastic union (forged when James VI of Scotland came south to become James I of England) into a functioning unitary state, with a single Parliament, Seal of State and economic coherence. Scotland retained her distinctive Church, education system and, perhaps most strikingly, legal system, but otherwise everything merged – including debts, which were absorbed by the English Exchequer, and of course the political elites, with 16 Scottish peers sitting in the House of Lords, and all future peers being denominated peers of Great Britain (as opposed to England or Scotland). If the elites were moderately enthusiastic, for geopolitical reasons if nothing else, lesser mortals betrayed less enthusiasm, and it took some time for the term 'Briton' to gain currency.[22] When George III declared, shortly after his accession in 1760, 'I glory in the name of Briton,'[23] the statement was viewed with consternation by his English subjects, who regarded it as an example of the pervasive and pernicious influence of his Scottish prime minister, the Earl of Bute. If the Scots were to prove in time by and large more enthusiastic about the Union, they remained then a nation very much divided by the immediate proposition of what appeared to be their effective absorption into their far larger neighbour. The Union was never as smooth as posterity (and the established Whig narrative) liked to portray it – a succession of Jacobite uprisings in favour of the Stuart dynasty puts pay to that reading – but it was in retrospect a good deal less disruptive than it might have been, and the Jacobites themselves have long since been incorporated into the 'romance' of Britain, such that Highland culture has come to be identified with Scotland as a whole in the popular imagination.

Be that as it may, the Glorious Revolution and its aftermath established the myth of Britain's political competence, especially when compared with the far more disruptive experiences of later European revolutions. The monarchy was not overthrown, but it was effectively restrained by the principle of parliamentary sovereignty along with a Bill of Rights that helped define the constitutional settlement. It may not have been a radical change, but it proved to be a durable one, and the fiction of hereditary succession even survived the somewhat dramatic transition to the Hanoverian dynasty in 1714 (George I was 51st in line to the throne, behind some 50 Catholic heirs who had been disbarred by Parliament and a great-grandson of James VI/I). The dominance of Parliament and the growth of the office of prime minister, the cabinet council and government as we would understand it today were further enhanced by the fortunate happenstance that the first two Hanoverian monarchs lacked competence or interest in English or British affairs.

Comparative political stability, encapsulated by the growth of parliamentary power and the rule of law, enabled a dramatic economic transformation of the country, with a series of 'revolutions' in science, agriculture, trade and industry, catapulting the new British state to become the first among the Great Powers by the end of the Napoleonic Wars in 1815. By this stage, of course, further Acts of Union had seen the Kingdom of Great Britain bound with the Kingdom of Ireland in a new United Kingdom. Then, in 1832, the widening of the franchise through the Great Reform Bill confirmed, if confirmation were indeed needed, that unlike her continental rivals Britain would be 'evolutionary' rather than 'revolutionary' in her politics. This was progress on an unprecedented scale, clothed in the ideas of the Enlightenment, which bore the promise of a more liberal age of social responsibility.

Looking back from the mid-19th century this spirit of progress had an air of inevitability about it, and Macaulay's history encapsulated that air of confidence. He may have been, as the historian Hugh Trevor-Roper described him, 'unquestionably the greatest of "Whig historians"',[24] but he was by no means the first and certainly not the last. Macaulay may have captured the historical mood, but he was building on a tradition stretching back to at least the 17th century that sought to identify the development of the legal and political rights of 'freeborn Englishmen' from the granting of the Magna Carta in 1215. This myth of (gradual) emancipation was so persuasive that it was soon adopted by Scottish Whig historians, not least, as noted above, David Hume, who considered it far more 'real' and beneficial than the various Scottish narratives of descent (the Declaration of Arbroath of 1320, an assertion of Scotland's independent sovereignty, was not considered at this stage to be of similar significance, and was in any case not as widely known). It was also widely admired abroad, not least by the French philosopher Voltaire, who contrasted the British parliamentary system favourably with the Bourbon absolutism that had stultified French political development.

The narrative was not, therefore, a wholly British conceit, and by the 19th century the exponential growth of the British Empire in all its varied manifestations seemed only to confirm Macaulay's confidence in the natural order of things. Indeed, the historian John Robert Seeley's famous adage that Britain appeared 'to have conquered and peopled half the world in a fit of absence of mind' suggests that this overseas expansion was not only inadvertent but also the consequence of a natural – unconscious – impulse.[25] This perception persisted notwithstanding the loss of the American colonies, which would have diminished lesser states.[26]

Macaulay, the quintessential Whig politician, in many ways represented the best of this impulse with his 'Minute on Indian Education' of 1835, in which he argued that the language of instruction in India should henceforth move to English to facilitate access to the new world of learning. Macaulay wrote: 'We have a fund to be employed as Government shall direct for the intellectual improvement of the people of this country. The simple question is, what is the most useful way of employing it?' Upon reflection, concluded

Macaulay, instruction in the English language would yield the best results:

> Whoever knows that language, has ready access to all the vast intellectual wealth, which all the wisest nations of the earth have created and hoarded in the course of ninety generations. It may safely be said that the literature now extant in that language is of greater value than all the literature which three hundred years ago was extant in all the languages of the world spoken together.[27]

Education was the key to self-empowerment, and Macaulay's educational reform, criticised by some, fraudulently rendered by others, was to have a profound impact on the development of the subcontinent.[28]

This 'civilising' impulse, which sought to remake the world in its own image, was never as high minded as Macaulay's example might lead some to believe, but it is difficult to overestimate the influence and impact of this particular narrative on generations of politicians, statesmen and intellectuals. However, such views were neither uncritically adopted nor evenly applied – the devil was always in the detail – and there was much that could be and was criticised in Britain's rule of India, from the 1788–95 impeachment trial of the first governor-general of India, Warren Hastings, on charges of corruption and maladministration, to the Amritsar massacre of 1919, which Winston Churchill, then the Secretary of State for War, condemned as 'monstrous'.[29] Dissent was one of the real strengths of British politics, and even Indians had occasion to comment on the enlightened nature of British rule.[30]

It was possible, for example, for Gandhi to have reflected in his youth 'that the British Empire existed for the welfare of the world'.[31]

If British statesmen fell short of the ideals they aspired to, and if the ability of the ruling class was decaying, they yet retained redeeming traits. In Orwell's terms: 'The English ruling class are *morally* fairly sound.'[32] As Orwell wrote, for all its faults, British democracy was 'less of a fraud than it sometimes appears'.[33] Arguably it was this moral imperative that persuaded Britain's leaders within the space of thirty years to enter two European wars in defence of the rights of small nations, in 1914 and 1939, and then in 1940 to 'stand alone' against what at the time must have appeared to be overwhelming odds. All this at considerable cost, in manpower and wealth, to itself.

To do so required a level of moral conviction and determination born of a Whig self-belief in the righteousness of Britain's cause as a champion of liberty, the firm conviction that Britain stood on the right side of history and the belief that she need only survive, in Churchill's words, to ensure the ultimate defeat of Nazi Germany. This belief in British exceptionalism (broadened during the war to include the United States and the parliamentary democracies of the English-speaking world) served Britain well at the time of her greatest existential crisis. But victory in two world wars also highlighted some of the dangers of this narrative of perpetual progress, most obviously in its 'inevitability'.

While Macaulay focused on a narrow period in history as the singular catalyst and cause of change, and others sought to investigate the constitutional and legal precedents, still more indulged too far in the temptation of tautological readings, placing the origins of British liberty in the Anglo-Saxon shire courts or 'moots' – a variation on the theme that Western civilisation was the product of a uniquely beneficial marriage between classical and barbarian (i.e. Germanic) cultures.[34] The consequence of this was to see even the most traumatic and disruptive historical encounters in a positive light, as having long-term benefits that ultimately yielded the exalted station the country found itself in. This was deterministic, 'inevitable' progress, which worked out well in the end and led inexorably to complacency and, at times, hubris.

Decadence and self-deprecation

The real danger of Whig history, as noted by Herbert Butterfield, its leading and most effective critic, was the whiff of inevitability: the idea that British supremacy and exceptionalism was predetermined, and could be left to its own devices seemingly absent from the decisions of individuals. Not only was this a flawed reading of history, its consequences for politics could be dangerous. It gave the impression that, aside from some details, the broad thrust (and direction) of English and British history was settled and uncontroversial, with a seemingly flawless grand narrative of ascent.[35] Indeed, the seemingly uncontested nature of British history stood in contrast to the vigorous, often poisonous debates on the continent and, more strikingly, in the United States, where challenges to the orthodox narrative (of 'Manifest Destiny') were more common. In Britain, the debate appeared to focus on the 'spoils of victory' rather than the 'causes of defeat', and as a consequence there was less rancour in the discussion. Even if Britain made mistakes, much as depicted in the 1943 Powell and Pressburger film *The Life and Death of Colonel Blimp*, they were considered well intentioned.[36]

Butterfield, despite his strong words, appears to have had a somewhat ambivalent relationship with Whig history. His criticism was emphatically of the methodological kind, recognising and warning of the dangers of such an ideological and sanitised view of history. But he also later appreciated both its impact and its broader value, along with the potential pitfalls of eradicating it altogether:

> It is not necessary or useful to deny that the theme of English political history is the story of our liberty... we are all of us exultant and unrepentant whigs. Those who, perhaps in the misguided austerity of youth, wish to drive out that whig interpretation (that particular thesis which controls our abridgment of English history) are sweeping a room which humanly speaking cannot long remain empty. They are opening the door for seven devils which, precisely because they are newcomers, are bound to be worse than the first.[37]

This of course is precisely what has happened. British political culture has long been a home to dissident views. It has been one of its strengths and, certainly from the 18th century onward, the ability to speak truth to power has been an aspect of political life on these islands that has been marked for admiration from abroad. It is one of the reasons, as noted above, that Britain has been such a refuge for political dissidents from overseas. Not that this fame for 'tolerance' should necessarily be misread for either consistent moderation – British politics has been subject to what Hume liked to call 'enthusiasm', like anywhere else – or indeed an attribute beyond general disinterest.[38] Orwell noted that in 1940, under threat of invasion, 'newspapers and pamphlets abusing the Government, praising the enemy and clamouring for surrender are being sold on the streets, almost without interference.' That this was so, he concluded, was less an act of tolerance – a conviction that 'freedom of speech' must be maintained – 'than from a simple perception that these things don't matter.'[39]

This complacency – one consequence of the 'gentleness' identified by Orwell and alluded to in the introduction to this volume – was to be complemented by another unfortunate characteristic: the reality that 'England is perhaps the only great country whose intellectuals are ashamed of their own nationality'.[40] The attribution to 'England' in this case is apposite insofar as England, being the largest of the constituent nations, was less anxious about the loss of its identity within Britain (and the UK) and its intellectuals more apt, by extension, to be self-critical. It goes without saying, however, that the juxtaposition of a critical, self-deprecating intelligentsia with a disinterested wider society might prove to be a toxic mix, especially in the event that the myth of progress received something of a shock to the system.[41] The Great War had been a shock to Western civilisation as a whole but Britain emerged victorious, even if financially ruined, with her imperial possessions intact and indeed extended. There were, in sum, reasons to be satisfied with the outcome, even if many people struggled to find them.

But the consequences of the Second World War were more complex. This was, if anything, the quintessential 'good' war, and at the very least necessary. Britain had experienced her 'finest hour', had 'stood alone', had emerged victorious but had also emerged diminished. In 1918, Russia was convulsed in revolution, and the United States retreated into isolation. In 1945, Britain was without any doubt the pygmy among the Big Three. Not only was she financially ruined and emotionally exhausted by the exertion of the war, but the United States had no intention of retreating into isolation and the Soviet Union, whose pact with the Nazis had bewildered Western Marxists, emerged from the war militarily and ideologically reinvigorated. Britain, meanwhile, was on the fast track to decolonisation, signalled emphatically by the granting of independence to India in 1947. This steady process of decolonisation was married to a thesis of decline, the reverse of the Whig narrative, for which it seemed the British were quite unprepared. Previously, neither the loss of the American colonies nor, perhaps most strikingly, the creation of the Irish Free State in 1922 – which, after all, signified the loss of some 20% of the territory of the United Kingdom at the time – had inaugurated such an intense period of self-reflection and self-doubt. But then, Britain's international stature was now under threat in a way it had not been before. It is perhaps no coincidence that Butterfield's original thesis gained traction after the Second World War.

There were of course reasons to be cheerful. The creation of the welfare state was a significant achievement (even if it ensured the continuation of a highly centralised state). It suggested that the Whig conviction of progress had not been wrong, and simply that the definition of what constituted progress had to change. Orwell had contended that the people of these islands were, at the end of the day, a family that came together in times of crisis – the only problem being that the wrong people had been in charge.[42] With the correct people at the helm, much could be achieved. Although the contemporary Left have taken encouragement from Orwell's analysis – and the fact that he considered himself a social democrat and a man of the left – they have been less enthusiastic about his repeated condemnations of the Left, who remained somehow immune to the pulls of patriotism (distinct in his view from nationalism), and whom he put on a par with the right-wing idiocy of those he characterised as 'Blimps'.

There were in Orwell's eyes two subsets of the middle class who were very much conjoined:

> One was the military and imperialist middle class, generally nicknamed the Blimps, and the other the left-wing intelligentsia. These two seemingly hostile types, symbolic opposites – the half-pay colonel with his bull neck and diminutive brain, like a dinosaur, the highbrow with his domed forehead and stalk-like neck – are mentally linked together and constantly interact upon one another...[43]

The dynamic between the aloof administrative incompetent and the aloof left-wing malcontent was to generate a highly destructive and degenerative cycle: a process alternatively known as decadence and decline.

What followed was a wholesale assault and deconstruction of the narrative of the past, for which its proponents were ill prepared, and for which they had no coherent response. The mood did not favour them, the politics of the country had swung to the left and the British Empire had not only become unfashionable, it had become an embarrassment. Perhaps more damning, it had become unaffordable. Locked in an ideological Cold War, Churchill's aspiration for an alliance between the English-speaking peoples and the Parliamentary democracies of the world fell victim to baser prejudices from both sides of the Atlantic. The problem with the 'special relationship' is that it enabled an intimacy that was unhelpful to either side. Americans balked at the incompetence of the Blimps and were determined to rid Britain of her empire.

The Left in Britain may have sympathised with America's ostensible anti-imperialism, but in turn regarded the United States as the harbinger of a much more dangerous capitalist hegemony that had made itself felt in what was perceived as America's rough handling of Britain's wartime debt in the immediate aftermath of the war. There was something curiously unjust, and not particularly 'special', about the treatment meted out to Britain. As if that were not enough, the British Left shared with the Blimps a distaste for American vulgarity. The Soviet Union on the other hand lacked that immediacy and comparable scrutiny, and thus basked in a strangely pristine majesty. For those avowed Marxists, the Soviet Union was an embodiment of progress through her realisation of the historical dialectic – and her scientific achievements, no less than her wartime exertions, proved it.

One of the consequences of this was a gradual whitewashing and effective rewriting of Britain's role in the recent war. This of course had its roots in the war itself, and in his 'first draft' of the history Churchill was acutely sensitive to the charge that Britain's commitment to the defeat of Nazi Germany and Japan was anything less than impressive.[44] The idea that Britain had simply kept the seat warm pending the arrival of the United States was an American interpretation that was matched by the belief of the Left that the real war had been fought on the Eastern Front by the Soviet Union, whose extraordinary casualties and suffering were sufficient evidence of sacrifice. (Any suggestion that Soviet resistance would have faltered without British and American help was ignored.[45]) As a result, British military achievements in North Africa – which were not insubstantial – were increasingly treated as a sideshow. More scurrilous were the dismissive attitudes towards Britain's stand in 1940; the military failures in France and the 'miracle of Dunkirk', which was credited to Hitler's apparent goodwill/incompetence; and the realisation, with hindsight of course, that the Battle of Britain was not a close-run thing at all.[46] All this was accompanied by a reassessment of that icon of the war, Churchill himself, whose failings – never far from the surface – were accentuated at the cost of his virtues.

Churchill in particular was emblematic of the very empire that was being decolonised physically and deconstructed mentally. In many ways, this was signalled by the British people themselves when Churchill was abruptly rejected at the polls in 1945 as an anachronism ill fitted to the needs of the future and the creation of the modern welfare state. He was dismissed as an imperial relic of the Victorian era, the epitome of Colonel Blimp. However unfair this characterisation may have been, and whatever affection he may have been held in personally, Churchill had come to be associated in the public mind with an era that they wished to put behind them. The British public had turned the page. All the ills of the past therefore were heaped on him, and there was little doubt that, for all his progressive pronouncements on the future governance of the world, it was his persistent defence of empire that provided his critics with all the ammunition they needed.

It is a matter of no little irony that the country that did most to diminish Britain's role in the world was the very country that was most enthusiastic about adopting Churchill as one of its own (the fact that Churchill had an American mother undoubtedly facilitated this appropriation). That Britain's role in the war and its imperial legacy were criticised by the Left should have surprised no one. That American political and intellectual culture played such a systematic role is interesting, all the more so because its approach was more nuanced and subtle. It was less to do with overt ideology and more to do with underlying myths. It was perhaps more effective because of the intimacy of the relationship Britain and the United States enjoyed and the fact that the United States was generally regarded as a partner and not an opponent to be challenged. As Britain shed its empire and retreated into economic instability, the shift in power to the United States became even more acute, and this was reflected in its cultural reach.

Churchill was right of course to emphasise the commonalities between the Great Powers of the English-speaking world. In general, British historians had tended to diminish the importance of the American Revolution as little more than an unfortunate argument between family members. There was a recognition that British policy had been heavy handed and ill thought out, and there were many admirers of the American cause in Britain – not least Edmund Burke. Indeed, outside the United States, the American Revolution (occasionally downgraded to a war of independence) was

viewed very much as a mere preamble to the far more consequential French Revolution that followed it. The French Revolution was a major event in European history, the harbinger
of modernity and nationalism. The American experience was
effectively relegated to a lower division of world events, as
befits a little local difficulty in a far-off land. Moreover, for all
the shock to the British political class, the American Revolution did not derail Britain's imperial expansion elsewhere – or
indeed in North America itself, where Canada continued to
expand westwards.

Needless to say, American historians were not so ambivalent. The American Revolution and the Founding Fathers
who authored it were part of the foundation myth of the
United States. This defining, seminal moment in its young
history would only swell in importance as the United States
grew in power. If Britain had Whig history, then the United
States possessed Whig history on steroids, underpinned by a
powerful myth of emancipation that drew on British history
and crucially identifying itself as 'anti-imperial'. This British
inheritance was disguised under a somewhat anachronis-
tic insistence on identifying all North American history as
'American', but the fact was that, crucially, this history did
draw on a narrative legacy that was Scottish and Irish as well
as specifically English.

Thus, American historians might trace their freedoms to
Magna Carta but their varied experiences argued for a distinct
trajectory of development. This distinction was crystallised
with the Revolution itself, which pitted the colonists against
a 'British' government that was regarded as distant and aloof
from its constituencies. Britain and the British Empire (along

with associated identifiers such as the redcoat), in this American narrative, became the villains of the piece, and continued to be so in popular American culture, reinforced by waves of immigrants from the margins of the British state – the politically and economically disenfranchised, with at best an ambivalent relationship to the state they had just left behind. What this meant was that the American myth of emancipation and ascent was curiously bifurcated, and the emergent American hegemony, first over the Western hemisphere and then as a global power, defined itself as anti-imperial. This was not an easy thing to achieve. But in an extraordinary narrative sleight of hand, the United States effectively inherited the mantle of British imperialism and, at the same time, transferred the guilt.

These ideas sat uneasily side by side, but the narrative of anti-imperialism, however incongruous it might look against the reality of American expansion, regularly dominated the interpretation, and certainly the rhetoric, of American power. Where it worked, such as in the Suez Crisis of 1956, it worked relatively well and the narrative gained credibility. But where it did not work, as in the coup against Mohammad Mosaddeq in Iran three years earlier, there was a distasteful haste to shift the blame onto Britain. The British in these cases were cast as being not only Blimps (i.e. incompetent anachronisms) but also unusually cunning in having duped their American cousins into the quagmire of imperial adventurism. For those on the left of the American political spectrum (and these things are always relative), such transferral offered a useful way to reconcile otherwise contradictory trends and enabled the cultural narrative of the British villain to take hold.[47]

Interestingly, given the English proclivity to switch between 'British' and 'English' at ease and with little sensitivity to the other constituent nations, the opprobrium likewise conflated the two, with British characters invariably being represented by English people and accents. The more upper class and effete the accent was the better, and, while this antipathy was never uniform, it was deeply ingrained and reinforced by certain communities – most obviously Irish-Americans. Above all it enabled a cultural trope that only gained in strength as American popular culture (most obviously, film and television) grew to dominate global markets and the English-speaking world in particular. Indeed, it became something of a joke that in the aftermath of the Cold War, and as the Second World War faded into distant memory, the British (English) provided a ready-made villain who would not be quick to take offence (it no doubt also helped that British actors spoke a language the Americans could understand, and provided a quality villain for a comparatively cheap wage).

More serious, however, was the rewriting of popular history. While there was a thriving indigenous film industry in Britain, the tendency of American studios to write out the British from the narrative of the Second World War was less consequential, and through to the end of the Cold War the British were at least represented, and often provided central characters. From the 1990s onwards, though, it would appear that in the wake of the Cold War's conclusion and the decline of British filmmaking the mood swung more emphatically towards American-centred narratives. In the case of *Saving Private Ryan* and its television offshoot *Band of Brothers* it was not so much a case of eliminating the British and their role as marginalising them to the point of extinction, such that it might not occur to the uninitiated that Britain had a significant role at all in the liberation of Europe. (That many of the roles in *Band of Brothers* – including the lead role – were filled by British actors is of course an irony that simply emphasises the complexity of the relationship.) In at least one film the British were written out of the script altogether, prompting criticisms, no less, in the House of Commons.[48]

Far more problematic were Hollywood's more 'subtle' historical assaults. These were not subtle in terms of the polemical revisions that were being presented, but as historical pieces they were regarded as less immediate and therefore less open to scrutiny and criticism. That is, 'history' provided scriptwriters with shelter and a considerable amount of dramatic licence. Perhaps the most notable of these cases was a pair of films starring Mel Gibson: one on the noted Scottish rebel and 'freedom fighter', William Wallace (*Braveheart*), the other on the American Revolution but broadly following a similar narrative arc (*The Patriot*). The latter, a sort of sequel to *Braveheart* with the 'fighting tyranny' narrative transplanted to North America, was a good deal less successful at the box office than the former, but together the pair provide the clearest indication of the transferability of the emancipation narrative, with a British (English) villain at its heart. In both cases, a reluctant rebel, who seeks nothing but a quiet life, is thrust into heroic rebellion by the brutality and injustice of his ostensible rulers.

In *Braveheart*, the 'redcoat' is replaced by the soldiers and mercenaries of Edward I, who is here presented as the

epitome of ruthless tyranny while his lieutenants are characterised by an admixture of craven loyalty and effete incompetence (variations on Blimp). The Scots are represented as
hangovers from a Pictish age, with Wallace and his compa-
triots covered in woad. The historical inaccuracies of the film
are too many to list here. Suffice it to say that this enormously
successful film (winner of the Oscar for the Best Picture of
1995) and its powerful narrative of emancipation enjoyed a
significant impact in Scotland itself, where Scottish nationalists appropriated the film for their own political purposes.[49]
Wallace had of course originally been appropriated to the
Scottish Unionist cause in the 19th century, as the man who
prevented conquest and therefore (in a somewhat awkward
argumentation) enabled the subsequent Anglo-Scottish
Union. This legacy was celebrated in bold architecture with
the Wallace Monument, erected by public subscription in
1869. In 1997, the car park to the Monument was endowed
with a new statue of Wallace in the image of Mel Gibson. The
sculpture was, unsurprisingly, a cause of great controversy in
Scotland, not least because no one has any idea what Wallace
looked like. The statue was finally withdrawn in 2008, and
subsequently failed to sell at auction.[50]

Far more consequential, in large part because the political
mood in Scotland had changed, was the television adaptation
of American author Diana Gabaldon's series of *Outlander*
novels, based around the Jacobite rebellion of Bonnie Prince
Charlie in 1745–6. The first series premiered internationally
in 2014 but was conspicuously not broadcast in Britain until
after the Scottish referendum in 2014, a decision alleged to
have been instigated by Prime Minister David Cameron for

fear of the programme unduly influencing the vote in favour of independence. The truth was, in all likelihood, more pedestrian than this rumour suggested, but its persistence was testament to the perceived influence of the series.[51]

The *Outlander* romance – and it is at heart a romantic story of the old school, with stereotypes laid on thickly – revolves around an English nurse who is visiting Scotland with her husband after the Second World War for a bit of rest and recreation when she becomes embroiled in a time-travel caper (by leaping into standing stones, no less) that thrusts her back to the 1743 Highlands.[52] There she meets a dashing young Highland warrior, who effectively becomes her true and undying love through a series of adventures both before and after the Battle of Culloden.

The series enjoys excellent production values and is highly entertaining, but the stereotypes and caricatures it presents would be a boon to any cultural studies seminar. The Scots are generally portrayed as hardy, noble warriors of the old school: down to earth, somewhat gruff but brimming with integrity and honour. They are the barbarians of the old school – the 'noble savages' of Rousseau's imagination – uncorrupted by the vagaries of modernity and the modern age. The English, on the other hand – also identified emphatically as British – have been corrupted by modern manners and wealth, and are presented by and large as effete. They are, in a word, decadent. The parallels with the mythology of the American Revolution should be immediately apparent.

The Scots are resolutely heterosexual and red blooded yet, importantly, respectful to the fairer sex. The English (British) are not respectful of much at all. Indeed, the series has been criticised for an excessive portrayal of sexual violence. Two characters are openly gay; one of them (a British officer) proves in time to be a sympathetic character, while the other, an aristocrat, is a deceitful idiot. A third character – Black Jack Randall, the main villain of the entire series and the ostensible ancestor of the heroine's modern husband – is a sexual pervert of extraordinary pretensions, with (unusually for modern villains) no redeeming qualities whatsoever. All three, incidentally, are attracted to the manly countenance of Jamie Fraser, the Highland hero and chief love interest of the series. Indeed, Randall is so attracted to him that he brutalises and rapes him. As a metaphor it leaves little to the imagination.[53]

The narrative arc is mythology of the first order, with a particular perspective rendered general and what is implied, or indeed left unsaid, as important as those points explicitly expressed. So, the backdrop to the series is a celebration of what amounts to the feudalistic idyll of clan life, where the Scots are Catholic, Gaelic speaking and, more importantly, essentially united against the Protestant modernity of the British state. The Scots after Culloden are a conquered people living under the yoke of the redcoat, and far from being partners of the English/British in union are just one more of their colonies. *Outlander* is a curious mixture of Irish and American mythology transplanted to Scotland, and a furthering of the romanticisation of Highland culture that began in, and was indeed encouraged by, a British state anxious to foster reconciliation. There is no hint here of the very real divisions in Scottish society, nor indeed of the sizeable contingent of Hanoverian loyalists of whom many fought as 'Britons' at Culloden.

None of this is to suggest that such cultural expression in film and television had a determining impact on political views within the United Kingdom.[54] At best, it has reinforced critical trends that were already taking shape in the post-war, post-imperial environment that was taking hold. But insofar as identity remains a work in progress, one that must be renewed and revitalised at regular intervals, popular expressions of this type had the effect of cultural attrition deployed against an identity whose value was being decried while its purpose was being taken for granted. Indeed, in the post-war period, an admixture of complacency and criticism enabled the gradual unweaving of the narrative thread of the nation and identity of Britain. As Butterfield feared, the deconstruction of Whig history resulted in its replacement by a narrative that was far less coherent and at times destructive.

The reassessment of Britain's role in the Second World War, and its relegation to second-tier status as befitted the realities of the post-war situation, was soon followed by a critical re-evaluation of imperial history. As Britons were being confronted by the realities of decolonisation – often more brutal than people were willing to accept – new histories were emerging from the peripheries, from the peoples of the British Empire themselves, offering critical new perspectives on the experience of empire. They were joined by critical and dissident voices within Britain itself that were anxious to reconcile with their past through a process of historical repentance and penance for the guilt of subjugation. There was much in this process that was important and valuable, since it rounded off a narrative that had in the past been too often a one-sided account. Imperial guilt was nonetheless cemented by Marxist readings of history, which provided a coherent narrative frame of reference in the space left open by the assault on Whig history.

'History' remained progressive, but the perceived destination was now quite different, and the British Empire was broadly seen by Marxists as but one stage on the road to a communist utopia. Britain and the British Empire (along with other European empires and the forces of capitalism in general) were understood to have fulfilled a role in the awakening of national liberation movements around the world – the essential precursor to final emancipation from capitalism itself.[55] But Britain was ascribed no particular moral purpose other than as a vehicle – although perhaps the most effective type – for the unfolding of the structural dynamic of world history. Of course, this structural reading of historical development had the added advantage of obviating responsibility. If historical processes were the consequences of structure, then agency became irrelevant and inconsequential. This was a highly simplistic reading of Marxist theory, but it served to reconcile and explain away imperial guilt. Marxist theory effectively squared the circle of cementing the guilt while allowing for a structural explanation. It could, in short, allow us to put our past firmly behind us, as long as everyone agreed on the destination.

Naturally, uniformity of opinion would never be the case. There were challenges to the attempted 'new orthodoxy', though these have remained deeply unfashionable, reflecting perhaps the political realities of decolonisation. A more balanced reading of imperial history seemed incongruous in light of the end of empire, and the real difficulties and often-brutal realities it exposed. The British Empire, as popular American culture would agree, was not a force for good but a repressor of local liberties.[56] It appeared at odds with the zeitgeist. But the fact that everyone clearly was not on board with the new Marxist interpretation of British history only ensured that its proponents argued it more passionately, leaning towards an ideological ferocity that was disconcerting in its totalitarian ambitions. It was no longer sufficient to decolonise the empire; one had to decolonise the mind, and if this entailed the deconstruction – and indeed destruction – of Britain, then so be it.[57]

Indeed, Marxist and post-colonialist historians viewed the very construction of the United Kingdom of Great Britain and (Northern) Ireland as a colonial project – beginning, of course, with Ireland, which increasingly became defined as the first 'English' colony, thereby backdating the colonial project as traditionally understood by several centuries, while at the same time conveniently ignoring the Scottish contribution to the settlement of Protestant Ireland. As in the best Whig history (in mirror image), the history of Anglo–Irish relations was abridged, simplified and narrativised as a colonial tale of oppression by Protestant settlers against the native Irish Catholics. There was of course sufficient truth in this idea, not least in the tragedy of the Irish potato famine of the 1840s, for it to gain traction. At the same time, the rough edges of the narrative were smoothed and refined to eradicate any contradictions that might exist, either to the myth of persistent and uniform Irish resistance to British rule, or indeed to the complex and often tortuous ways in which successive British governments sought to reconcile the conflicting interests that existed in Ireland. The immediacy of the problem was of course brought home in the 1970s during what was euphemistically termed the Troubles in Northern Ireland, the latest iteration of the sectarian struggle that had plagued the Irish, during which it was swiftly forgotten that British military intervention had been initially triggered in support of the Catholic minority and not the Protestant majority.

The Irish contingent in this longstanding conflict, and in its latest manifestation in Northern Ireland, has benefitted in material and ideological terms from American support. The large Irish diaspora in the United States was swiftly able to garner sympathy from ordinary Americans raised on a steady diet of antipathy to the British Empire and the redcoat while at the same time retaining an admiration for the 'English'. It is worth pausing here to reflect on how the complex semantics and terminology of the United Kingdom and its myriad names allowed individuals to simultaneously both like and dislike Britain/England/the UK by simply according them different names. (It was of course possible to admire the British while detesting the English, though given the association of Britain with empire, this was less frequent.) Nevertheless, the simplification of the Anglo–Irish narrative as the continuation of – or prequel to – a colonial struggle was handsomely reinforced by supporters in the United States.

This Americanisation of the Irish struggle would be followed by a further transferral to Scotland, where nationalism, although never far from the surface, began, particularly in the latter half of the 20th century, to enjoy a resurgence in contradistinction to the English. If the Welsh might justly be aggrieved by their conquest at the hands of the English, and the Irish by the British plantations, the Scottish rendition of the narrative was a good deal more complex and contradictory, not least because there was something acutely Scottish about being British. All the peoples of these islands had at times in their history been willing participants in the economy and politics of the Empire, even the Irish. But the Scots had perhaps been the most enthusiastic participants of all.[58] There is a reason, after all, that the Empire was British rather than English.

Nonetheless, in a feat of impressive semantic agility, Scottish nationalists sought to distance themselves from the Empire by resituating the 'British' as a distinct 'other' outside their revised narrative of descent. This despite the fact that the modern political construct of Great Britain had in many ways been a Scottish idea that the English had viewed with suspicion. Now, however, as elegantly rendered in the television series *Outlander*, the Scots too had become victims of an imperial aggression that – much like the aggression suffered by their Irish cousins – came in redcoats, was Protestant and was ignorant of local customs and identities. This was given immediate political resonance by a cultivated perception of electoral politics as being unrepresentative of the people of Scotland. In popular political mythology, Caledonia had indeed become Hibernia.

By situating Britain, the British Empire and now the British state beyond their immediate responsibility, the Scottish and Irish nationalists had unwittingly enabled the emergence – or re-emergence – of the last and perhaps the most potent of the local nationalisms: English nationalism.

A heady mix of post-colonial narratives had come home, with an emphasis on local identities and self-identifying. This was combined with and reinforced by a Marxist ideology that empowered and invigorated resurgent – and indeed insurgent – nationalisms that had hitherto been suppressed (and contained) within a broader British narrative framework. The seams appeared to be coming apart in an ideological project hell-bent on a process of 'creative destruction', whose collective goal and intent was to throw everything out so as to start anew and, on the ashes of the old, build something better.[59]

It was a curiously revolutionary and romantic turn for a people hitherto apparently unimpressed by the prospect of political upheaval. This potent mix of nationalism and revolutionary socialism was handily reinforced and assisted by the sheer ineptitude of British policy – the perennial Blimps of popular lore. The Blimps were not immune to the underwhelming sensation of decline after the moral highs of the Second World War, and their efforts to manage the process were at best mixed and at worst grist to the mill of those who sought to rewrite the narrative entirely. The first of many calamities was the debacle at Suez in 1956. But to this can be added the disastrous invasion of Iraq in 2003 and, arguably, Brexit in 2016. All three events can and have been characterised as exercises in imperial hubris and nostalgia, though the proponents of the last of these were probably driven more by the buccaneering spirit of Elizabethan England than any enthusiasm to recreate Clive of India. Nonetheless, these events, and many lesser ones in support, convinced critics and the many people who for a variety of reasons were willing to listen that Great Britain and the 'British state' could not escape their imperial past, that they had become decadent and redundant and that, consequently, the only solution was their dissolution.

The battle for 'Britain'

The criticisms currently being levelled at the British state are, of course, not being raised for the first time in history. Britain has been subjected to such accusations before. American colonists arguing for their independence were keen to identify the metropole – the heart of the Empire and the imperial administration in particular – as corrupt and beyond redemption. Why else seek to break free? In seeking to establish and restore their rights as 'freeborn Englishmen', the colonists argued that the British state had lost its way and had become a tyranny. As a means of reconciling the contradictions that may arise in its approach, the arguments were focused on particular aspects that had corrupted the whole, whether attributing the blame to Parliament or, more effectively for political purposes, the person of the King himself. In this way, the animus could be targeted and the general protected, renewed and reimagined as a 'republic of laws', albeit on a different continent.

Orwell had similar if distinct concerns in 1940, at a time when the British state arguably faced its greatest existential crisis. For Orwell, the ruling class was then in decline, and if it was not inherently malign, it was yet curiously ineffectual and impotent. This was a different type of decadence – a far more serious one in many ways, because it lay unrecognised. This was the tyranny of complacency, and what was urgently needed was a period of renewal of the body politic in its entirety.

In both cases, of course, the state (and society) rose to the challenge, and a period of renewal did arguably take place. There were reserves of moral conviction to draw upon, revise and revisit. But if victory in 1945 ultimately served to provide this conviction with a boost, the narrowness of the margins of success in that period should not be underestimated. Churchill's leadership undoubtedly served to rescue a situation that was dangerously close to compromise and moral collapse, but the effort required to win the war likewise drew on reserves that were already in short supply. The navel gazing that was to follow did little to renew the spirit of the state, with criticism soon eliding into self-deprecation and, on occasion, loathing.

Here we should pause and reflect on the meaning of the term 'decadence'. In common usage it tends to relate to excessive wealth, but, as it was originally conceived, wealth was but one aspect of a much more corrosive political and moral decline. For our purposes, it may be summed up in one word: complacency. In this sense, Orwell's criticisms are more relevant to our purposes. Some 18th-century writers charting the rise and fall of civilisations, notably Edward Gibbon, interpreted 'decadence' as an explanatory tool for decline. According to Gibbon and others, the 'Persians' represented the epitome of this process in action – though in 18th-century Europe it was the French (and the Bourbon court in particular) who were most keenly identified with this process. For Gibbon, identifying the Persians as decadent meant that they could be categorised as civilised and not barbarian in the traditional – Germanic – understanding of that term. Persian barbarism was of a different kind, and resulted from what was in effect 'over-civilisation': an excess, not only in wealth, but in etiquette, rules and regulations – in sum, governance. This was crucially tied to a sense of complacency, a belief that the situation both was inevitable and had achieved a pitch of perfection beyond which it was impossible to do much more – or, indeed, to change. In other words, the sense of inevitability was accompanied by an air of fatalism.

Decadence, in the moral sense in which it was originally conceived, combines within it a curious admixture of 'pride' and 'fall'. Orwell's characterisation of the situation in which the British state found itself in 1940 echoes this description and is a clear clarion call to the body politic to respond to the challenge, but it is also – and this is a crucial distinction often omitted by his more left-wing supporters – an acknowledgement that there is much that can and must be salvaged, that a lackadaisical attitude to moribund decline should not be the dominant motif of the British state that, for all its flaws, has much to commend it. Indeed, if the post–Second World War Blimps sought to manage decline and settled into an ideology of declinism,[60] the intelligentsia (not all in this case necessarily left wing) settled into a process of deconstruction that was further enabled and empowered by advances in technology (the mass and social media) along with a dangerous decline in professionalism that saw the power and authority of 'moral judgment' gradually withdrawn from the individual.

The decline of the 'professional' (the specialist, in contemporary parlance), which in earlier days might have been characterised as the decline of the 'gentleman', and all this implied by way of an attitude and approach to life, was facilitated both by the growing ability of the state to intervene in the everyday process of administration and management, but also by the changing nature of education (the rise of the technocrat and the decline of responsibility) and the technological empowerment of information over knowledge (facilitated by the internet and, above all, social media).[61] In a paradox of rare beauty, the intelligentsia have succeeded in creating a political culture of anti-intellectualism, which has simply fed this depreciating cycle.

As noted above, the British state and its antecedents have previously been the subject of vigorous, sometimes vicious, criticism. But the scale and speed of the recent onslaught and the lack of a coherent response – or indeed the means of a coherent response – have affected and hindered the ability to renew. Not only do we face an excess of information, but we have deprived ourselves of the means to process this into meaningful knowledge. The mass media therefore imparts information that is often too easily and uncritically absorbed by a receptive public that is unable and ill equipped to engage with it. Meanwhile, the rise of the technocrat and the decline of responsibility has converged with an increase in the political culture of 'rights' to ensure that everyone is now a protected minority (one might now self-identify to degrees hitherto unimagined) and everyone has become a victim of their political environment and cultural inheritance – in sum, the state. We have taken that which had meaning and purpose and, through excess of application, have rendered it vacuous and empty. This is the peculiar form of decadence that we have inflicted upon ourselves.

And nowhere is this more obvious than in the realm of

history, not only in its popular manifestation but in the academy, where the multiplicity of different genres and approaches has hollowed out the grand narratives of old and replaced them with the 'seven devils' so feared by Butterfield. The result is a degree of historical vacuity and illiteracy rarely experienced and made all the worse by the fact that the knowledge that is produced is more heavily influenced and shaped by ideological prejudice than ever before. It may be that Whig history was narrative myth at its best, but we appear to have replaced it with narrative myths at their worst. These are at best highly sensitive to the most constructive criticism and at worst devoid of meaningful context. Indicative of the sorry state to which we have fallen is the current preoccupation with 'values' as a descriptor of identity. 'British values' are frequently characterised as enjoining such ideas as democracy, human rights and freedom of speech, though there is rarely any context provided for these terms and no sense of how these values might have been reached and/or achieved. Designed in part as a means of fostering integration, they have been justifiably criticised for a lack of distinction, context and, most interestingly, for actually contradicting British values in being unnecessarily prescriptive! The real genius of the British spirit in this understanding is that it precludes definition, and that – much like the unwritten constitution that has shaped British politics – our collective identity is fluid and organic.

We might compare our current somewhat haphazard and incoherent attempts with the efforts by Macaulay in India, where, as previously noted, he established an educational system designed to empower the Indians with the knowledge of the West and to draw them nearer to the identity of the British. But how was this identity to be defined and shaped? In educational terms, what constituted the knowledge necessary to approach the world as an Englishman or a Briton? The curriculum that was subsequently devised covered a variety of emerging disciplines including history, geography and literature, and it was this curriculum that was subsequently adapted back to Britain as political reform and the widening of the franchise necessitated the 'education of our masters'. There were no doubt many criticisms that could be made of the detail, but the point was this: 'values' were not imparted free of any context or contingence, they were imbued with meaning.

One of the curiosities of our current predicament is that in deconstructing and debunking the Whig narrative of exceptionalism we have failed to recognise that these developments, for all their apparent flaws, remain contingent. The Whig narrative, as Butterfield only too effectively showed, contributed to a sense of inevitability and complacency, a sense that exceptionalism was somehow inbred, and was a structural – or even biological – certainty. But we have effectively thrown the historical baby out with the methodological bathwater, and in arguing for a lack of exceptionality we have removed any distinctiveness that might imbue *value* to Britishness. Thus the development of democracy is regarded by many as wholly unexceptional and quite normal in terms of historical development. Such a perspective holds that democracy may be an achievement, but it is a general one, which the British may have reached earlier than others, but which has been predetermined by some natural unfolding of history (in the ideal or material terms described by Hegel and Marx). This ironically reflects the conceit of some Western political historians who regard liberal democracy, with all its associated accoutrements, as the inevitable endgame of history, adding for good measure that those states that have somehow not achieved this enviable situation suffer from a historical abnormality, which must and should be rectified.

The truth of course may be somewhat more sanguine: that the distinctive political development experienced by some – though by no means all – Western countries has been contingent on particular historical experience, which may by all means be replicated (it may indeed be desirous to do so), but which is neither inevitable, structurally determined nor achievable in the absence of agency. This is not to argue that the benefits accruing from such a system of government must be denied to others, but to recognise the historical vulnerability of these processes and outcomes, that the development of civilisation (to use the traditional term) or modernisation (to use its contemporary equivalent) are neither unilinear nor unidirectional.

Significantly, this was a reality that was understood by the practitioners of Whig politics rather than the interpreters of Whig history. If we returned to our sources and looked at the way in which Britons presented their country's remarkable political and economic achievements to visitors from abroad, we would be struck by the implicit humility that characterised their words. The growth of British power in the 18th century was presented not as a series of military victories, but rather as a consequence of the application of new forms of governance, the rule of law and the gradual extension of education.

These provided the anchors and the ballast of the new state – democracy, in our understanding of the term, was rightly subservient to the idea of the 'republic' as a state founded on laws by which the monarch was constitutionally delimited. This provided stability for a commercial and trading society to flourish and expand, which in turn defined and shaped attitudes. None of this 'progress' was presented at the time as inevitable, but rather contingent on historical experience and decisions made by individual actors and institutions. These skills could be transferred, but the process could also be reversed or could break down. The concept of decline – and, indeed, decadence leading to decline – was well known and appreciated by the writers of this period, whose proximity to an earlier age of instability had made their appreciation of achievement all the more acute.

Edmund Burke was perhaps the first political thinker to articulate the precariousness of the present, when he compared the delicate, organic growth of the British constitution to the trauma then afflicting France, noting that stability might only be restored through the barrel of a gun and the firm hand of a military leader. Creative destruction was a romance best left to the imagination and not inflicted upon society at large. Burke would have been the last to suggest that the political system he inhabited was perfect – far from it, as indicated by his own criticism of the handling of the American colonies, and of (arguably far more consequential) the government's failure to fulfil the promise of the 1801 Act of Union with Ireland by providing for a measure of Catholic emancipation. Had alternative decisions been taken in either case, the history of these islands would have been markedly different – if not better, then certainly not worse. But, at the same time, the decisions that were taken cannot be wholly laid at the door of the government or the principal political actors without reference to the myriad pressures and influences that weighed on their minds.

The American Revolution was fought against a principle that many might have considered reasonable, that the colonies be asked to contribute through taxation to their own defence – a defence that had been paid for to the Americans' own extensive interest and gain in the French and Indian War some years earlier. The 'tyranny' of George III, so much the focus of American revolutionary anger, appears in retrospect to be much exaggerated. Even contemporaries were perplexed at the grievance that had been manufactured. Some even mocked the claim that all men were created equal, in light of the retention of slavery.[62] The truth of the matter was that, far from acting in an unconstitutional manner, George III was by his own account fighting to protect the rights of Parliament, and it was against Parliament, not the king, that the American colonists were most vexed. When John Adams (who would later become the second president of the United States) was appointed the United States' first ambassador to the Court of St James's, he approached the throne with trepidation only to find that this supposed ogre of a monarch was only too keen to be the first to welcome the friendship of the new United States.

Moreover, the American colonists did not present their grievances as 'Americans' – there was arguably at the time no such identity – but as 'freeborn Englishmen' whose natural rights had been transgressed. However, once again, this did not necessarily mean that they identified themselves as ethnic Englishmen; a good many would not have regarded themselves as such, but would have felt that their worldview and attitudes could be identified as such, and that their political and ideological pedigree could be thus defined and historically traced. This of course was thoroughly Whiggish in perspective, tracing back to the Glorious Revolution of 1688, the Bill of Rights of the following year and still further to the founding document of 'English' emancipation, the Magna Carta. It is worth remembering that the Magna Carta was probably more revered and popularised among the American colonists and their descendants than among the English or the wider British community that would inherit it.

Indeed, the myth of emancipation (or liberty) that has emerged is in significant part a product of American rather than British history, and unsurprisingly it is among the latter that the narrative of emancipation has come under the greatest scrutiny and deconstruction. Not least, of course, in the case of Magna Carta, which has been reduced by British historians to a baronial extraction of concessions from a King who promptly ignored its provisions. Butterfield himself provided a succinct exposition of the myth in *The Englishman and His History*, noting that the Great Charter was effectively rediscovered during Parliament's struggles with the Crown in the lead-up to the English Civil War (alternatively titled the War of the Three Kingdoms, given the involvement of Scotland and Ireland in the hostilities), and was provided with a historical pedigree that was as much invented as real. Indeed, the charter that really did appear to matter was the expanded version of Magna Carta that was reissued by Henry III – a fact often elided from the myth of Magna Carta's origin with King John, which was established some time later.

There can be little doubt that the embellishment of the importance of Magna Carta has done much to encourage its subsequent diminution and relegation to the historical margins. But there is also little doubt that in comparative terms the concession in Magna Carta that no man would be arbitrarily imprisoned – albeit within the context of feudal law – was to prove a significant milestone that would be built upon and then interpreted by later jurists, most importantly Edward Coke in the early 17th century. From a modern perspective, these developments might appear small and incremental, but in the context of their time, they were crucial steps in the development of common law, trial by jury and – by the late 18th century – the right to the provision of a legal defence. Moreover, taking a comparative perspective, both regionally and globally, these developments and the struggles they encompassed – because it is important to remember that rarely was progress achieved without both struggle and sacrifice – provided a distinctive historical inheritance to the peoples of these islands.

Indeed, as the legal arguments of Coke and the subsequent struggle of Parliament against the Crown were to show, none of these developments were inevitable, and none were achieved without considerable bloodshed. The Civil War that traumatised the Three Kingdoms in the middle of the 17th century was among the most violent periods in the history of these islands, framed by a poisonous legacy of sectarianism and radical populism. It is only when we begin to recognise the cost that we can begin to appreciate the value of what was achieved. The same is true of the Glorious Revolution of 1688 and the Bill of Rights that followed. Again, it must be right to criticise the apparent inevitability of a process that was inherently contingent, but that criticism should not diminish the consequences that resulted.

Three successive developments, all perhaps more contingent on and consequent to accident than design, served to shape the constitutional settlement and foundations of the country: these were the Glorious Revolution, the Act of Union of 1707 and the Hanoverian succession in 1714. All were intimately related and all reinforced a distinct constitutional trend, which saw the relationship between Crown and Parliament shift decisively in favour of Parliament. This may not have been immediately apparent – material and ideological changes are rarely synchronised, and it takes time for the consequences of actions to take hold – but clear trends can be discerned, and the frame of action had been set. Thus, the Glorious Revolution established, and the Hanoverian succession confirmed, that the principle of hereditary monarchy through primogeniture was for all intents and purposes dead. Britain – Scotland was party to this decision both before and through the Act of Union – effectively opted for an elective 'hereditary' monarchy, in which Parliament had the final decision on who might inherit the throne and, crucially, Parliament could choose to remove a monarch considered an affront or a danger to the 'constitution'. The fiction of hereditary monarchy was of course retained for presentational purposes, and thenceforth the notion of a 'divine right' to rule was replaced by a monarchy that served at the will of the people as represented through Parliament. Churchill perhaps put it most succinctly when he told the exiled Duke of Windsor, 'When our kings are in conflict with our constitution, we change our kings.'[63]

This shift in emphasis from Crown to Parliament was confirmed by the Hanoverian succession and the granting of the crown to a very distant relation of the sitting monarch on the basis of religious preference. Defining this as a Protestant succession should not disguise the fact that one of the reasons it was regarded as preferable was very simply because Catholicism was associated in the public imagination with absolutism. Religion was very much a political issue. To regard it simply as a matter of sectarian prejudice is to miss the point altogether and, crucially, to read our current prejudices into the past – as Butterfield would have warned against.

Nevertheless, this act of design was further assisted by the accident that the first Hanoverians were neither particularly interested nor conversant in their new kingdom, with the vital consequence that the practice of government effectively devolved upon ministers, resulting in the development of the office of prime minister. None of this represented a radical break or dramatic change, but it shaped a process that grew organically and allowed the institutions to shape and be shaped by their environment. The material substance of institutions is reinforced by ideational alignment that over time cements the change and makes it a 'fact of life'. This symbiotic relationship is crucial for understanding how the British state and constitution have grown. It is not simply a case of bricks and mortar, but also of ideas.

Much the same can be said about one of the most dramatic changes that was conceived, planned and implemented: The

Act of Union in 1707, merging the two kingdoms of England and Scotland, which had been bound in dynastic union for over a century, into a single kingdom named Great Britain. Unsurprisingly, this 300-year-old Union has come under increasing scrutiny as a result of the rise of the Scottish National Party and the demands for independence among some sections of the Scottish population. Emotionally, much of this appears to be driven by a popular 'abridgement' of Scottish history that conveniently conflates the medieval wars of independence (*Braveheart*) with the Jacobite uprisings of the 18th century; the latter was a rising in favour of a Stuart dynasty whose great political project was of course the creation of Great Britain. Once again, one can dismiss the more extreme version of Whig history that regards the Act of Union as both natural and inevitable. But nor can the Act of Union be seen as a feat of conquest imposed on Scotland by an imperial England.

There have been three occasions when Acts of Union have contributed to the creation of the modern British state. The 1536 Act of Union with Wales formalised the reforms of Thomas Cromwell in the 16th century and was clearly the consequence of conquest. The Acts of Union with Ireland in 1800 can also be seen as the consequence not only of attempted conquest but a measure of colonisation. In both cases, there were clear attempts at integration at the political and economic level if not the social – though the Acts of Union with Ireland proved the most flawed in this respect due to the failure to include Catholic emancipation, arguably one of the most serious mistakes made by the British state, in this case (and in contrast to the debacle over the American colonies) in the guise of the Crown rather than Parliament. But the 1707 Act of Union was something quite different, and its imposition was as much on the English as it was on the Scots. The dynastic union under the Stuarts of Scotland, despite its length, had not led to the sort of social and political union that James VI/I had hoped for – even though the fact that the 'English' Civil War originated in a dispute between Charles I and his Scottish subjects, and came to embroil all three kingdoms, suggests that the links were more intimate and immediate than the formal politics suggested.

Be that as it may, the brief parliamentary union that was imposed by Oliver Cromwell during the interregnum was swiftly reversed in the Restoration, and the renewed attempt to secure this at the turn of the 18th century proved no less controversial. That this was effectively contrived and implemented by an aristocratic oligarchy driven in many ways by the geopolitical foresight of the first Duke of Marlborough – whose victories against the French in the war of the Spanish (or indeed English) succession made the entire process possible – should not detract from either its effectiveness or desirability. There was opposition in both countries to the proposed merger, but there was also significant support, and if the balance of political power appeared to lie with England, the economic terms were generous to Scotland. Indeed, one of the striking aspects of the Union was the centrality of economics and the forging of what we might today term a single market and customs union, above all other aspects. In many ways, the architects of the Union focused their attention on the economic foundations, leaving the political and social aspects to develop organically around that basis. So, curiously, this single kingdom would retain two systems of law and education, and distinctive religious hierarchies. It was in many ways a traditional pre-modern union with a thoroughly modern economic foundation. Anchored in the past, it looked confidently towards the future.

Critics coalesced around an affinity for the old Stuart dynasty, and came from all corners of the new kingdom as well as Ireland. They tended to be, though were not exclusively, Catholic, and were most concentrated in the Scottish Highlands and among the Tories in England. They represented in many ways a very strange alliance of interests, but the Jacobites were not fundamentally about Scottish independence. They were more about a different type and style of government, with some arguing against the more centralised government emerging under the Hanoverians, and others against that centralisation in a unified Parliament. Of the three main rebellions in 1689, 1715, and 1745, arguably the most serious – and the one that has enjoyed the most romantic appeal – was that of 1745 under the leadership of the 'Young Pretender', Charles Edward Stuart. However, 'Bonnie Prince Charlie' was interested in becoming the king not of Scotland, but of Great Britain. The rebellion eventually faded because of a lack of traction in both England and, ultimately, Scotland, where many lowland Scots regarded the rebellion as no more than mischief. It is often forgotten that there were Scottish regiments fighting on the government side when the Jacobites were defeated at Culloden.

The fact that the rebellion was enabled at all was the consequence of a British defeat at the Battle of Fontenoy the previous year, during the War of the Austrian Succession – in which, as it happens, Scottish regiments were fighting on behalf of the Crown. The Duke of Cumberland was widely lauded by the cities of Edinburgh and Glasgow and awarded an honorary doctorate for his efforts by the University of Glasgow.[64] The prefix 'butcher' was initially accorded him by English Tory opponents for the brutality with which he suppressed the revolt after the battle – though this suppression is often conflated with the Highland Clearances, the causes of which were more economic than political (reflecting the decline and fall of feudalism), and were initiated before the rebellion of 1745, reaching a crescendo long after the Union had been cemented. Indeed, on the contrary, one of the most striking things about the Jacobite rebellions is not how quickly they subsided but how rapidly their romance was integrated, as with the Scots in general, into the political romance of Great Britain.[65] A young Edmund Burke observed in the immediate aftermath of Culloden:

> 'Tis strange to see how the minds of the people are in a few days changed. The very men who, but a while ago, while they were alarmed by his progress, so heartily cursed and hated those unfortunate creatures, are now all pity, and wish it could be terminated without bloodshed.[66]

George III even went so far as to provide a pension to the exiled Jacobite heir through a sense of familial duty.

If the first half of the 18th century was fractious, the second half moved quickly to realise the potential of the Union, with Scots showing themselves to be far more enthusiastic about Britain than their English counterparts. It is remarkable that many of the icons of British identity that we today take for granted were crafted by Scots, including the figure of John Bull (Scottish satirist John Arbuthnot originally conceived of Bull as the archetypal Englishman, with a Scottish sister called Peg), and the poem that formed the basis for the lyrics of Britain's unofficial anthem *Rule, Britannia* – wrongly assumed to be a boast rather than an exhortation. The lyrics of *Rule, Britannia* were not originally intended to be a claim to empire but a demand that Britain rule the waves to protect against foreign invasion (in doing so obviating the need for a strong standing army, which many at the time saw as the root to despotism).[67] The song is therefore more indebted to the great intellectual transformation of the 18th century, the Enlightenment, than it is to empire.

Indeed, as historian Linda Colley points out, the connection between the formation of Great Britain and the foundation of empire is incidental rather than causal:

> In retrospect, these successive phases in the forging of Great Britain and then of the United Kingdom can be viewed as having (among many other things) laid a secure basis for the expansion of Empire. But the causes at the time of these various phases of union should not be confused with the eventual cumulative effects of union.[68]

Indeed, all the constituent 'nations' of the Union – including after 1801 the Irish – proved to be willing participants in and contributors to the imperial project that was emerging in diverse fields, be they economic expansion, political administration or military exertion. There is a reason it was the

'British' rather than 'English' empire. Macaulay, the author of the Whig narrative, stands as a good example of a Briton of Scottish descent participating in empire as a quintessentially Enlightenment project – a civilising project, if you will, one that sought to bring the benefits of good governance and the power enabled by knowledge.[69]

This of course would be a sanitised reading of empire and its consequences. Even Macaulay was motivated in part by a sense of intellectual – and by extension 'civilisational' – superiority and, needless to say, Great Power rivalry was rarely altruistic. But it is likewise important to recognise that the Empire was not driven simply by economic avarice and the exploitation of the other, nor by an unequivocal sense of superiority. The British Empire – this 'chaotic conglomerate', as John Darwin memorably describes it[70] – could not have been sustained in the absence of an overarching, binding authority, and, while it may be unfashionable to say so today, the Empire could not have survived had many of the subject peoples not invested in some way or form in the British ideal. British Indian (volunteer) armies fought with distinction in both world wars. When German academics protested at the deployment of Indian troops against them on the Western front, the response from a prominent group of British academics (the following extract being given sufficient length to show the contrast in approaches) was clear and emphatic:

"If it were possible," writes Prince Bülow, who directed German policy as Imperial Chancellor from 1900 to 1909, "for members of different nationalities, with different language and customs, and an intellectual life of a different kind, to live side by side in one and the same State, without succumbing to the temptation of each trying to force his own nationality on the other, things on earth would look a good deal more peaceful. But it is a law of life and development in history that where two national civilisations meet they fight for ascendancy. In the struggle between nationalities one nation is the hammer and the other the anvil; one is the victor and the other the vanquished." No words could indicate more clearly the cause that is at stake in the present war. They show us that there are still governments in Europe so ignorant as to believe that the different nationalities of mankind are necessarily hostile to one another, and so foolish and brutal as to think that national civilisation, or, as the German Professors call it, "culture," can and indeed must be propagated by the sword. It is this extraordinary conception which is at the back of protests like that of Professor Haeckel and Professor Eucken (men whom, in the field of their own studies, all Europe is proud to honour) against "England fighting with a half-Asiatic power against Germanism."

There are not only half-Asiatics, there are real Asiatics side by side with England; and England is not ashamed of it. For she does not reckon the culture of Europe is higher than the culture of Asia, or regard herself as the hammer upon the anvil of India.[71]

This was in sum not an empire forged or retained through military force alone. When force was used, it was used selectively, often inadequately and occasionally not at all. This was not a consequence of altruism; there should be no doubt that the British imperial authorities when roused to anger could be as brutal as any power, and incompetence was of course never far from the surface. But the incompetent and rash use of coercion was frequently condemned – if not by the authorities, then by the myriad dissident voices that did exist.

Moreover, the use of force was infrequent because it was expensive, and the British government hated spending money on imperial (ad)ventures that some in the political establishment considered wasteful. Indeed, the British ambivalence to empire was noted by foreign observers – even the objects of British imperialism – and found puzzling. Britons as a whole were far less interested in and far more critical of empire than their imperial possessions and commonwealth would suggest.[72] This ambivalence, one might add, extends to this day with respect to the Union itself.

For many, what bound the imperial idea together was the belief in good governance and the administration of justice.[73] For example, a contemporary of Macaulay, Lord Glenelg (another Scot), argued:

> British rule in India should be conducted on "the great and just principle" that "considerations of wealth, of commerce, of revenue should be as nothing compared with the paramount obligation" to consider the interests of the Indians and promote "the welfare and prosperity of that great empire which providence has placed in our hand".[74]

This was of course founded on the Whig narrative of liberty and emancipation, and the variations of the theme that subsequently emerged.

The application of British justice and the spread of common law proved to be a powerful force for imperial cohesion, and nowhere is this more apparent than in the great human tragedy of empire, slavery and the transatlantic slave trade. The focus on slavery today might lead some to think that the British Empire invented the practice and was solely responsible for its continuation. As with most assessments there is little or no comparative analysis other than to point to the fact that the British Empire abolished the slave trade well before the United States abolished the practice altogether. Most will probably only be aware of that fact from cinema – most obviously, the American film, *Amistad* (1999).

But what is striking is that common law made no provision for slavery whatsoever, and when a case of an escaped slave was brought to court in England in 1772, Lord Chief Justice William Murray, Earl of Mansfield (yet another Scot) ruled:

> The state of slavery is of such a nature, that it is incapable of being introduced on any reasons, moral or political; but only positive law, which preserves its force long after the reasons, occasion, and time itself from whence it was created, is erased from memory. It's so odious, that nothing can be suffered to support it, but positive law. Whatever inconveniences, therefore, may follow from the decision, I cannot say this case is allowed or approved by the law of England; and therefore the black must be discharged.[75]

Although Mansfield later sought to qualify his decision, its impact on wider society cannot be underestimated, and it was regarded as a landmark ruling by abolitionists. It was however limited to Great Britain and did not apply to the trade or the wider British Empire. It would take another generation for William Wilberforce to convince Parliament in 1807 to abolish the slave trade, and another 27 years (until 1834) for the act abolishing slavery to take effect.

None of this should serve to justify what remains a grotesque stain on British history, nor should we idealise the impact of the law. Torture was never formally part of common law either, but it was certainly practised. Nevertheless, when the British Empire is viewed through a comparative lens one can agree with Gandhi that it did aspire to a moral purpose even if it frequently fell short of these ideals. British justice was not universally regarded as unduly harsh nor governance unduly oppressive. The governments it replaced (some of them, not least that of Mughal India, empires in themselves) were rarely if ever paragons of enlightened virtue and were frequently held only to standards far below those expected of the British. (Slavery was of course widely practised beyond the European world, and Europeans were often victims of slave raids from North Africa.) Even the contemporary European empires had far less to commend them. One need not search hard to find atrocities committed in the Belgian Congo; the French enjoined a brutal colonisation of Algeria; and the process of decolonisation in these empires was often more protracted and traumatic than that experienced in the British Empire (where the Commonwealth arguably stands as testament to a comparatively smooth transition). Indeed, many

British subjects eager for independence recognised that their chances of achieving such an outcome with the minimum of violence were far better with the British than they were with the self-styled Japanese liberators during the Second World War. We should never forget that Gandhi, the epitome of an Indian nationalist, was a Middle Temple lawyer, well versed in the traditions of the common law.[76]

Renewal

Napoleon commented that 'the moral to the physical is as three to one'.[77] This essay has sought to investigate the moral and ideological bases for British identity: the ideas behind the structure, the moral cement that we have done our best to erode. It is often assumed that institutions are physical structures – buildings and organisations – but, as Burke correctly analysed, the basis lies in the collected ideas inherited and reinforced from the past. In a word: tradition. The French philosopher Montesquieu described this as 'virtue' without which no 'republic', no state founded on the principle of the rule of law, could survive. The focus here has been on historical narratives – the ways in which English and then British history has been narrated, challenged and deconstructed, especially in the post Second World War period, when it came under rigorous attack from a variety of scholarly and popular sources, and turned in on itself in a manner that was arguably unprecedented in recent memory. Part of this has been a consequence of the transformation in the mass and social media that has resulted in the democratisation of information at the expense of knowledge. But it also reflects a self-loathing that Orwell recognised only too well in 1940.

Britain has long been famous for its liberalism and its dissent. It is these two characteristics that have made it both attractive and welcoming to the unorthodox and free thinkers who found themselves unwelcome elsewhere. But even those who admired these British ideals understood that at the heart of the British political compact lay a harmony within which dissent operated through implied convention. The boundaries of these traditions of conduct may be tested but not broken – at least, not with the blithe abandon that amounts to the 'creative destruction' so fashionable in some quarters. For those familiar with the consequences of such political romanticism, such reckless enthusiasm reeks of decadence. In some quarters at least, liberalism as an ideal has been transformed into liberalism as an ideology, and it has become no less sanctimonious than the (religious) orthodoxy it seeks to overthrow.

Foreign observers, curious as to the causes of Britain's success in managing its political affairs, have perhaps been more acutely aware of this political compact, and have understood the care with which British politicians have tampered with or sought to change conventions that have otherwise served them well. Above all, a balance must be achieved between what you withdraw from a system and what you invest to reinforce it. If you take out more than you invest, then you find that your political, no less than your economic, infrastructure may in time be found wanting, and may be less able to withstand the shocks that are bound to afflict it. Indeed, the success of the British state since its inception has less to do with an inherent political placidity than with the inherent strengths that have enabled it to withstand, sustain and overcome a series of shocks that would have overturned lesser states. It has been an ability to manage crises, to recover and renew, that has distinguished Britain from many of its contemporaries. The oceans have never been calm; the British ship of state has simply been more robust.

But material structures have only accounted for part of this strength, and, I would argue, the lesser part, the greater coming from conviction and a measure of self-belief that remains vital because of the diverse challenges Britain faces. That these challenges can be robust and critical is in large part due to the general recognition that the architecture is both clear and based on strong historical foundations. The competition that exists between the constituent parts of the United Kingdom (exemplified in many ways in sport) provides a model by which competing nationalisms can be harnessed to the collective good and the welfare of all. The same is true of the confrontational nature of political debate, much mocked and increasingly abused but in many ways central to the implicit dialectic of the British state, which allows for ideas to be challenged, refined and re-defined.

We should turn away from the personalisation of government and 'celebritisation' of politics in which the strategic and thoughtful is sacrificed to the immediate and popular. Not all traditions are worthless, nor all conventions pointless; there is a reason we address the office and not the individual. Only then might we begin again to see not only the cost of everything but the real value of those things that are fundamental to our collective being. The United Kingdom of Great Britain and Northern Ireland is a uniquely successful political union, but it requires a collective effort, not least from the English, who for too long have approached this achievement with a calculated and studied air of neglect. If Englishness has been characterised by a mentality that all are invited to invest in, then, looking forward, the English too must recognise and publicly appreciate (not just in times of crisis) the importance and value of the collective identity that is Britishness: a British identity that serves to bind a series of ethnicities – now far more diverse than the original constituent nations – around a civic culture of shared values and aspirations. This can only be achieved through a programme of public education, and it will not be easy.

The British state, whether by accident or design, contains within it the mechanism for regular renewal, but only if the parameters are understood and the foundations robust. Both these aspects have come under increasing attack with little general appreciation of the consequences. To address these issues, we need to reacquaint ourselves with our history – a *British* history, not an English history with Celtic appendages – and educate ourselves on the foundations of our constitution in order to understand, warts and all (as opposed to the current tendency of 'warts and *no* all'),[78] the context of these developments as historical phenomena: not exceptional but contingent; bound by an 'emotional unity'; shaped by a shared experience, culture and, perhaps most underestimated, a language of rare international reach and influence.

Britain's is not a narrative of inevitable progress, as Whig history has suggested. But the ideas that shaped radical Whiggism in the 18th century undoubtedly informed opinion and sought, to a greater or lesser extent, to drive policy both at home and abroad. One could argue that Whiggism shaped by the progressive ideas of the Enlightenment was the founding political myth of the British state, conceived as a means of binding hitherto distinct peoples into a commonwealth for the welfare of all. These principles in many ways informed Britons' sense of themselves, however inadequate to the task they may have been in practice. Perhaps most importantly, the people of these islands were acutely aware that what might be acquired – through the application of education, discipline, industry and above all the rule of law – might also be lost. That they too, in the language of the time, had emerged from a 'barbarous' state to engage fully with what they understood to be 'civilisation' – a state of being identified not with any group, 'race' or people, but with a *process* of development that must by definition remain a work in progress. It is a lesson we would do well not to forget.

Notes

1   G. Orwell, 'The Lion and the Unicorn', *Why I Write*,
     London, Penguin, 2004, p. 29.

2   George Mikes' book *How to be a Brit*, first published
     in 1946, springs to mind, as do the filmmaker Emeric
     Pressburger (Hungarian, like Mikes) and Fritz Spiegl
     (an Austrian immigrant), who composed BBC Radio
     4's *UK theme*. Spiegl's theme – incorporating traditional
     tunes from the four constituent countries, framed by
     renditions of *Rule, Britannia* – marked the switch from
     the BBC World Service to Radio 4 every morning, and
     was controversially cancelled in 2006 by the then-
     controller of Radio 4, Mark Damazer, on the grounds
     that listeners would prefer an extra slot of news. For
     details, see 'The UK Theme', *BBC Radio 4*, http://www.
     bbc.co.uk/radio4/history/uk_theme.shtml (accessed 14
     February 2018).

3   With apologies to Orwell, though the reader will soon
     discover my debt to him throughout this text.

4   G. Orwell, op. cit., p. 17. Perhaps the best visual
     expression of this tendency is shown in the Powell and
     Pressburger film of 1943, *The Life and Death of Colonel
     Blimp*, when the German character, Theo, explains his
     reasons for seeking refuge in Britain.

5   One side sees the contradictions within, while the other
     side is better able to compare the contrasts without;
     both tend to smooth out the rough edges in the creation
     of their narratives.

6   G. Orwell, op cit., p. 23.

7   M. Daly, 'Ireland: The politics of nomenclature', *These
     Islands*, 13 December 2017, http://www.these-islands.
     co.uk/publications/i279/ireland_the_politics_of_
     nomenclature.aspx.

8   G. R. Searle, *A New England?: Peace and War 1886–1918*,
     Oxford, Oxford University Press, 2004, p. 8; L. Colley,
     Acts of Union and Disunion, London, Profile Books,
     2014, p. 17. According to Colley, the acronym 'UK' only
     became relatively widespread in the 1970s.

9   Searle, op cit., p. 8.

10   On the plasticity of the term 'Briton' see L. Colley,
     Britons: Forging the Nation, 1707–1837, New Haven,
     Yale University Press, 2012, p. xvii.

11   G. Orwell, 'Antisemitism in Britain', *Essays*, London,
     Penguin, 2014, p. 284.

12   See M. Billig, *Banal Nationalism*, London, Sage, 1995,
     p. 5. If nationalisms remain latent at the core, they
     nonetheless exist.

13   One colleague has wryly noted that he has a novel in
     him in which first the Scots leave the Union, followed
     in rapid succession by England and Wales, leaving only
     Northern Ireland as the last remnant of the 'United
     Kingdom'!

14   C. Kidd, 'Ethnicity in the British Atlantic World,
     1688–1830', in K. Wilson (ed.), *A New Imperial History:*

Culture, Identity and Modernity in Britain and the Empire, 1660–1840, Cambridge, Cambridge University Press, 2004, p. 261.

15 The term '1707 Act of Union' conventionally encompasses the two acts passed in 1706 and 1707 by the parliaments of England and Scotland, respectively, to put into effect the Union of their countries. The term can be understood as such throughout this essay, unless the context indicates that I am referring to only one of the two acts.

16 C. Kidd, *Subverting Scotland's Past: Scottish Whig Historians and the Creation of an Anglo-British identity, 1689–c.1830*, Cambridge, Cambridge University Press, 1993, pp. 101–215.

17 C. Kidd, 'Ethnicity in the British Atlantic World', p. 277.

18 Searle, op cit., p. 12. This is not to deny the existence of casual prejudice in England or Britain. See, for example, G. Orwell, 'Antisemitism in Britain', pp. 278–287.

19 Churchill, in his speech to Harvard University in 1943 on the unity of the British and American peoples, argued: 'Let us go forward in malice to none and good will to all. Such plans offer far better prizes than taking away other people's provinces or lands or grinding them down in exploitation. The empires of the future are the empires of the mind.' See 'The Gift of a Common Tongue', *International Churchill Society*, https://www.winstonchurchill.org/resources/speeches/1941-1945-war-leader/the-price-of-greatness-is-responsibility (accessed 14 February 2018).

20 The United States, which takes 'from the many, one' (*e pluribus unum*) as a de facto national motto, can be considered the child of the Whig enlightenment.

21 See G. Orwell, 'The Lion and the Unicorn', p. 15. Orwell notes that the British (or, in his terms, English) are in the habit of sleepwalking into disaster. See also P. Hennessy, *The Kingdom to Come*, London, Haus Publishing, 2015, p. 75.

22 See S. Saunders Webb, *Marlborough's America*, New Haven, Yale University Press, 2013, p. 579. Saunders Webb argues that the War of the Spanish Succession is misnamed and that the proper name should be the War of the English Succession, since it was Marlborough's defeat of Louis XIV and his cultivation of the Scottish peers by awarding the Scots a 'disproportionate share of military commands' (p.151) that ensured the success of the Act of Union.

23 N. Harding, *Hanover and the British Empire, 1700–1837*, London, Boydell and Brewer, 2007, p. 183

24 H. Trevor-Roper, 'Introduction', in Lord Macaulay, *The History of England*, London, Penguin, 1986, p. 7.

25 J. R. Seeley, *The Expansion of England*, Chicago, University of Chicago Press, 1971, p. 12.

26 The damage to Britain of losing America was minimised not least by the diplomatic aplomb of the very king the Americans had grown to detest. Indeed, for all the fractiousness of the early relationship between Britain and the United States, there was a common heritage and perhaps a common future that would overcome it.

27 T. B. Macaulay, 'Minute by the Hon'ble T. B. Macaulay, dated the 2nd February 1835', *Frances W. Pritchett, Columbia University*, http://www.columbia.edu/ itc/mealac/pritchett/00generallinks/macaulay/ txt_minute_education_1835.html (accessed 14 February 2018). The policy was actually implemented by the governor-general of India, William Bentinck.

28 Notably, Macaulay's reforms have been the subject of wide misrepresentation online through a falsified quotation that regularly circulates on social media. See A. Mitra, 'The Infamous Macaulay Speech That Never Was', *The Wire*, 19 February 2017, https://thewire. in/110263/macaulays-speech-never-delivered.

29 For more on the tension between principle and practice, see J. Darwin, *The Empire Project: The Rise and Fall of the British World-System, 1830–1970*, Cambridge, Cambridge University Press, 2009, p. 180.

30 See, for example, S. Ahmed, 'Speech of Sir Syed Ahmed at Meerut [1888]', *Frances W. Pritchett, Columbia University*, http://www.columbia.edu/itc/mealac/ pritchett/00islamlinks/txt_sir_sayyid_meerut_1888. html (accessed 14 February 2018).

31 D. Gilmour, *Curzon*, London, John Murray, 1994, p. 166.

32 G. Orwell, 'The Lion and the Unicorn', p. 37. Italics are from the original.

33 Ibid., p. 27.

34 For a rendition of this argument, see David Starkey's Channel 4 TV series *Monarchy*, broadcast in 2004.

35 H. Butterfield, *The Whig Interpretation of History*, London, W. W. Norton & Company, 1965. See also M. Billig, op. cit.

36 Notably, Churchill had deep reservations about the film, not only because of its depiction of a sympathetic German officer (albeit an anti-Nazi one) but because of the naivety of the lead character who, some have argued, Churchill seems to have thought might be a criticism of himself. See M. Lee, 'The Life and Times of Colonel Blimp: why Churchill wanted it banned', *The Telegraph*, 15 June 2012, http://www.telegraph.co.uk/culture/film/classic-movies/9334436/The-Life-and-Times-of-Colonel-Blimp-why-Churchill-wanted-it-banned.html

37 H. Butterfield, *The Englishman and His History*, Cambridge, Cambridge University Press, 1944, pp. 3–4. Significantly, this 'review' of the thesis was published at the height of the war – a moment of 'supreme crisis'.

38 D. Hume, 'On Superstition and Enthusiasm', in *Selected Essays*, Oxford, Oxford University Press, 2008, pp. 38–43; G. Orwell, 'The Lion and the Unicorn', p. 20.

39 G. Orwell, 'The Lion and the Unicorn', p. 29.

40 Ibid., p. 40.

41 See P. Hennessy, op cit., p. 9.

42 G. Orwell, 'The Lion and the Unicorn', p. 29.

43 G. Orwell, 'The Lion and the Unicorn', pp. 37–8.

44 W. S. Churchill, *Their Finest Hour*, London, Weidenfeld & Nicolson, 2015, pp. 20–22.

45 G. Orwell, 'Notes on Nationalism', *Essays*, London, Penguin, 2014, p. 315.

46 See, for example, J. Ferris and E. Mawdsley, 'The war in the West, 1939–40: The Battle of Britain?', *The Cambridge History of the Second World War: Volume I*, Cambridge, Cambridge University Press, 2015, pp. 315–16.

47 A good example of this narrative arc can be seen in the 'Iran' episode of Granada Television's *End of Empire* series, broadcast in 1985.

48 'U-Boat Film an "affront", says Blair', *BBC*, 7 June 2000, http://news.bbc.co.uk/1/hi/uk/781858.stm. See also *Hansard* HC Deb 7 June 2000 col 283.

49 'What Braveheart did for Scottish independence', *Medievalists.net*, 20 August 2014, http://www.medievalists.net/2014/08/braveheart-scottish-independence.

50 'Wallace Statue back with Sculptor', *BBC*, 16 October 2009, http://news.bbc.co.uk/1/hi/scotland/tayside_and_central/8310614.stm.

51 'David Cameron "met Sony over UK Outlander release"', *The Scotsman*, 20 April 2015, http://www.scotsman.com/lifestyle/culture/tv-radio/david-cameron-met-sony-over-outlander-uk-release-1-3747339. The series was broadcast in the United States and Canada in August 2014 and in Ireland in October 2014, but not in the United Kingdom until March 2015.

52 As a fantasy one might describe it as *Brigadoon* on steroids. Interestingly, the Scottish nationalist politician George Kerevan describes it as 'Brigadoon meets Doctor Who'. See G. Kerevan, 'Patriotic propaganda is

the order of the day for the British establishment', *The National*, 27 November 2017.

53 One of the hallmarks of the series is the literary trope of 'rape and ravishment', and it is not always clear where one ends and the other begins. In this respect, the narrative echoes and reverses the slanders against the Earl of Bute in the 1760s. See L. Colley, *Britons*, pp. 122–3.

54 Although it would appear that the film *The Darkest Hour* has convinced at least one supporter of Scottish independence to switch allegiances back to the United Kingdom. See 'The Darkest Hour – A Film that Changed my Mind', *The Wee Flea*, https://theweeflea.com/2018/01/24/the-darkest-hour-a-film-that-changed-my-mind/.

55 The defining text in this respect was Lenin's *Imperialism: the Highest Stage of Capitalism*, published in 1917. See J. Darwin, 'Decolonization and the End of Empire', in R. Winks (ed.), *The Oxford History of the British Empire: Volume V: Historiography*, Oxford, Oxford University Press, 1999, p. 541.

56 This was not necessarily the prevalent view in more traditional American political circles, where the perpetuation of British power was regarded as an essential buttress to the United States – even if this meant the continuation of imperial commitments.

57 On the impact of post-colonial theory, see D. Kennedy, *The Imperial History Wars*, London, Bloomsbury, 2018, pp. 7–21. See also R. Hyam, *Understanding the British*

Empire, Cambridge, Cambridge University Press, 2010, p. 15.

58 The Scots also have their own dedicated volume in the *Oxford History of the British Empire* book series. See J. MacKenzie and T. Devine (eds.), *Scotland and the British Empire: Oxford History of the British Empire Companion Series*, Oxford, Oxford University Press, 2011.

59 A dominant voice in this regard has been Tom Nairn. See T. Nairn, *The Break-Up of Britain*, London, Verso, 1977. Nairn has since been criticised for abandoning Marxism in favour of nationalism. See N. Davidson, 'In perspective: Tom Nairn', *International Socialism Journal*, http://pubs.socialistreviewindex.org.uk/isj82/davidson. htm (accessed 14 February 2018).

60 See R. Tombs, 'The myth of Britain's decline', *The Spectator*, 8 July 2017.

61 See, for example, S. Kovach, 'Former Facebook exec feels "tremendous guilt" for what he helped make', *Business Insider*, 11 December 2017, http:// uk.businessinsider.com/former-facebook-exec-chamath-palihapitiya-social-media-damaging-society-2017-12.

62 T. Hutchinson, 'Strictures upon the Declaration of the Congress at Philadelphia in a letter to a Noble Lord, etc', *Online Library of Liberty*, http://oll.libertyfund. org/pages/1776-hutchinson-strictures-upon-the-declaration-of-independence?q=hutchinson# (accessed 14 February 2018). With thanks to Henry Hill for drawing this to my attention.

63 D. Cannadine, *In Churchill's Shadow*, London, Allen Lane, 2003, p. 50.

64 The University of Glasgow went so far as to fund a company of soldiers for the Crown in 1745. See H. Smith, *Georgian Monarchy: Politics and Culture 1714–1760*, Cambridge, Cambridge University Press, 2009, p. 176.

65 Hannah Smith argues that 'although the Jacobites had lost the past', by the 19th century, 'in historiographical terms they were well on the way to winning the future'. H. Smith, op. cit., p. 3.

66 P. Langford, *A Polite and Commercial People: England 1727–1783*, Oxford, Oxford University Press, 1998, p. 211.

67 For a literary history of the anthem, see R. McLean, 'James Thomson and "Rule Britannia"', in G. Carruthers and C. Kidd (eds.), *Literature and Union*, Oxford, Oxford University Press, 2018, pp. 79–96.

68 L. Colley, *Britons*, p. xxv; Hyam, op cit., p 16.

69 The interesting debate here, of course, is how investment in this 'ideal' effectively sowed the seeds of the Empire's dissolution, as education led to self-empowerment and then self-government.

70 Quoted in Hyam, op cit., p. 19.

71 Greenwood, Seton-Watson, Wilson and Zimmern, *The War and Democracy*, London, Macmillan, 1915, p. 5.

72 Hyam, op cit., p. 15.

73 See Curzon's comments on the purpose of government in India, in D. Gilmour, op. cit., p. 166. See also Hyam, op cit., p. 24; Greenwood, Seton-Watson, Wilson and Zimmern, op. cit., p. 90.

74 Hyam, op cit., p. 26. For Hyam's assertion that 'if it was not an ethical *empire*, it was not an empire without an ethical *policy*', see p. 31 of the same volume.

75 E. Heward, *Lord Mansfield: A Biography of William Murray 1st Earl of Mansfield 1705–1793 Lord Chief Justice for 32 years*, Chichester, Barry Rose, 1979, p. 141.

76 Chandrika Kaul writes: 'After independence Indians borrowed 250 articles from the Government of India Act (1935) for their new constitution, and chose to run their army, railways, press, broadcasting, judiciary and parliamentary system substantively on British lines. Prominent nationalist leaders extolled the virtues of British imperialism.' See C. Kaul, 'Were Empires a Force for Good?', *BBC World Histories*, issue 3, Mar–Apr 2017, p. 36; G. Orwell, 'Reflections on Gandhi', *Essays*, London, Penguin, 2014, pp. 459–466.

77 There are variations on this quote depending on the translation, but it comes from his notes of 1808 titled 'Observations on Spanish Affairs'. An alternative translation reads: 'In war, three-quarters turns on personal character and relations; the balance of manpower and materials counts only for the remaining quarter.'

78 A phrase used by John le Carré after having viewed an early draft of Adam Sisman's biography. See A. Sisman, *John le Carré: the biography*, London, Bloomsbury, 2015, p. 15.